IN THE TIME OF TRIAL

Two Plays For Lent Or Good Friday:
The Face Of Jesus
Pontius Pilate And The Dreams Of Claudia

BY HENRY SCHOLBERG

C.S.S. Publishing Co., Inc.
Lima, Ohio

IN THE TIME OF TRIAL

9317 / ISBN 1-55673-570-7   PRINTED IN U.S.A.

These plays are dedicated
to my grandchildren —
all of them.

Preface

The Face Of Jesus and *Pontius Pilate And The Dreams Of Claudia* tell the story of the last moments of Christ on earth.

The Face Of Jesus has Christ confronting Barabbas at close quarters. They are in the same cell. They are the good and the bad, the holy and the profane, and they are face to face. They clash. One of them is triumphant in an unspectacular ending.

It is a "what if" play that asks, "What if Jesus and Barabbas had been in the same cell while the crowd outside was yelling, 'Crucify Jesus!' and, 'Release Barabbas!' "

We know, of course, that they never shared a cell. But, what if . . . ?

Pontius Pilate And The Dreams Of Claudia looks at the story with the eyes of Claudia Procula, the wife of Pilate. Pilate is having trouble remembering this prophet from Galilee. "We had them crawling out from every rock," he says. But Claudia remembers well, and she jogs her husband's memory until he sees the blood on his own hands.

Like *The Face Of Jesus*, this play is historically impossible. Caiaphas is talking to Pilate in the procurator's palace. No Jew of Caiaphas' standing would have allowed himself to set his feet inside a pagan building.

It was not the author's intent to rewrite the Holy Scriptures in either of these plays. He is protected by the unwritten permission contained in the expression "dramatic license."

I am deeply indebted to my wife, Phyllis, who helped me with the proofreading of these pages.

Henry Scholberg

The Face Of Jesus

A One-Act Play
For Lent Or
Good Friday

Program Notes

This play is based on an event that never took place. We know from what we read in the gospels that when Pontius Pilate offered the people a choice between Jesus and Barabbas, the people demanded that Barabbas (who was under sentence of death) should go free and Jesus be crucified. So Jesus went to his destiny and Barabbas to his oblivion — the two of them never meeting.

In this play we ask: If Jesus and Barabbas had been put in the same cell for about half an hour, what would they have had to say to each other? How would they have related to each other? Would Barabbas have said, ''I'll have nothing to do with Jesus; he is a holy man?'' Would Jesus have said, ''I will have nothing to do with Barabbas; he is an evil man?''

Or would they have reached out to each other: Barabbas to Jesus out of a sense of guilt, and Jesus to Barabbas in a spirit of love?

The Face Of Jesus

(This is a one-scene, one-act, two-character play: Jesus and Barabbas being the two characters. The scene opens in a prison cell with two cots. Barabbas is seated on his cot. If the actor is musically inclined, it would be appropriate to have him strumming a guitar or amusing himself with some other musical instrument of some sort. Suddenly Jesus enters, tripping and falling as though he had been shoved violently into the cell.)

BARABBAS: Hey, High Pockets! Why don't you pick on someone your own size? . . . Creepo! . . . Yeah! Your mother's one, too. *(To Jesus.)* Aw, pick yourself off the floor. We all have to around here.

JESUS: I must have tripped.

BARABBAS: Don't make excuses for him. Just because he's nine feet tall, he thinks he can push everybody around. When I — I mean, if I ever get out of this hell hole, I'm going to put my hands around that guy's throat and strangle him.

JESUS: He was only doing his job.

BARABBAS: Making excuses for him again, huh?

JESUS: Well, I admit he may have been a little over-zealous. *(Jesus starts to sit on the wrong cot.)*

BARABBAS: No. That's your bunk over there.

JESUS: Terrific.

10

BARABBAS: You sure talk funny.

JESUS: I wasn't aware of that. I wasn't trying to be funny.

BARABBAS: I mean, you don't talk like the rest of the cons who end up in death row.

JESUS: Death row?

BARABBAS: Yeah. There's just four of us here. You don't play bridge, do you? Golf? Tennis? We could get up a foursome some lazy afternoon.

JESUS: Who are the other two?

BARABBAS: A couple of buddies of mine who got caught stealing. Just thieves. By the way, what are you in for?

JESUS: I'm not sure.

BARABBAS: You mean, you're innocent? Welcome to the club.

JESUS: I think it's called aggravated conspiracy to cause dissension. Something like that.

BARABBAS: Aggravated conspiracy to cause dissension. That's a new one. I wonder who dreamed that one up.

JESUS: The church.

BARABBAS: The church?

JESUS: Uh-huh. *(Pause)*

BARABBAS: Well?

JESUS: Well, what?

BARABBAS: Aren't you going to ask me what I'm in here for? We generally do that, you know? We ask each other what we're in here for.

JESUS: I know what you're in here for.

BARABBAS: Oh? Well, then suppose you tell me.

JESUS: Murder.

BARABBAS: Right so far.

JESUS: Sedition.

BARABBAS: Right again.

JESUS: Arson.

BARABBAS: You're on a roll.

JESUS: Rape.

BARABBAS: That's not what I called it, but that's what the prosecutor called it. Anything else?

JESUS: Isn't that enough?

BARABBAS: I suppose it'll do for the present. Oh, by the way, my name is Jesus.

JESUS: So is mine.

BARABBAS: My old man's name was Abbas; so I'm Jesus Bar-Abbas. But I'm usually called Barabbas. Who's your old man?

JESUS: I am called Jesus Bar-Joseph.

BARABBAS: So your father's name was Joseph, huh?

JESUS: He wasn't my real father.

BARABBAS: Oh. Then Joseph is your stepfather, and your real father is dead.

JESUS: There are some people who believe that.

BARABBAS: Why do you look at me like that?

JESUS: I look at you the way one looks at a friend.

BARABBAS: No. That's not it. Contempt.

JESUS: Hardly contempt.

BARABBAS: Pity. That's it: pity. Well, don't waste your pity on me, Jesus Bar-Joseph. I don't need your pity. I've led a pretty full life. I've drunk my share of wine, I've killed my share of men, and I've had my share of women. I see you shaking your head. Okay. So it's not pity. Self-righteous. Try that on for size. You're self-righteous because you have a lesser crime. What was it?

JESUS: Aggravated conspiracy to cause dissension.

BARABBAS: Whatever. Well, let me tell you something: You'll hang the same as I will, and when they take us down, we'll be just as dead. You want some words of comfort? They say you get used to hanging if you hang long enough.

JESUS: I believe that's called gallows humor.

BARABBAS: You're still looking at me. But I can't figure out that look. Not contempt. Not pity. Not self-righteous.

JESUS: Try compassion.

BARABBAS: Don't even know what that is.

JESUS: Do you know what love is?

BARABBAS: Yeah, but my definition of love probably ain't the same as your definition of love.

JESUS: You must have loved your mother.

BARABBAS: Sure. But I wasn't the only one.

JESUS: Tell me about her.

BARABBAS: Well, let me put it this way: I'm not sure who my father was — except that he's supposed to have been a guy named Abbas; so I had only one father. But I had a lot of uncles — if you get my meaning.

JESUS: I get your meaning.

BARABBAS: What about your mother?

JESUS: My mother is a sweet lady who wrapped me in swaddling clothes and laid me in a manger.

My mother is a young woman who goes to the office every morning, sits behind a typewriter, takes dictation and makes coffee for her boss.

My mother is a woman who cleans house for her family, washes their sheets, mends their socks, cooks their meals.

My mother is a teacher who stands in front of 27 children all day and teaches them their spelling and multiplication tables.

My mother is a woman in Russia who works all day in the field or the factory or the roadway.

My mother is a woman in Africa who tries to give suck to her baby, but can't because her breasts are shriveled and dried up. She herself doesn't have enough to eat.

14

My mother is the little sister in a far away home for old beggars and lepers and the derelicts of society. She holds their hands and gives them love as they die.

My mother is the widow who still mourns the loss of her dear husband. She, too, is my mother.

BARABBAS: How about the lady who sits on a bar stool with a drink in her hand and says: "Hiya, Handsome! New in town?" Is she your mother?

JESUS: Yes, and I have forgiven her.

BARABBAS: What about my mother? Is she your mother?

JESUS: Yes.

BARABBAS: Then, does that mean that you and me are brothers?

JESUS: I'll let you answer that one.

BARABBAS: You and your damn riddles. You're crazy. You know that, don't you?

JESUS: There must be many who think so.

BARABBAS: You come in here claiming to have two fathers and umpteen mothers and making excuses for High Pockets. Yeah, you gotta be — hey! I think you're just crazy enough to try it. Let's escape.

JESUS: There is no escape for either of us.

BARABBAS: Yes, there is. I'll go back into my life of crime, and you'll go back to whatever it is that you do best. It's the oldest trick in the book, but old High Pockets is just dumb enough to fall for it. This is how it works. I've seen it a million times on the late-late show. You pretend you're sick, see? Start gagging or croaking or something. I call out to High Pockets that a prisoner is dying. That'll bring him. They don't like us to die on them. It means forms to fill out and all that. Messy. They like everything neat and tidy. They prefer doing their own killing. It's regulation, you know?

So here's how it works. You start gagging and choking like you're Jimmy Cagney. I yell bloody murder. High Pockets comes rushing in — you're not listening — He comes rushing in, looks at you lying on the floor, and I overpower him like this. *(There is a struggle.)* Sorry about that. I get carried away sometimes. What was that word you used?

JESUS: Over-zealous.

BARABBAS: Whatever. Anyway, I overpower him, kill him, grab his keys and then set my friends free and all four of us make a run for it. One of us is bound to make it.

JESUS: There is no escape for any of us.

BARABBAS: What's to lose? We're all going to die on the cross, anyway. There you go, looking at me again. Where did you say you were from, Jesus Bar-Joseph?

JESUS: Nazareth.

BARABBAS: I'm from a small town not far from here. You probably never heard of it.

JESUS: Try me.

BARABBAS: Bethany.

JESUS: I know where that is. I have some friends there.

BARABBAS: Nazareth, huh? Jesus — Nazareth. That's it! You're Jesus of Nazareth. I've heard of you. You're the preacher! Hey, guys! My cellmate is a preacher. Well, you don't preach at me, Preacher.

JESUS: I never preach at anyone.

BARABBAS: No? Then, what do you do?

JESUS: I speak the truth.

BARABBAS: Yes. I know about you. Love your neighbor. Love your enemy. Isn't that about it?

JESUS: There's one more: love your God.

BARABBAS: And then there are those parables. We heard about your parables. How did that one go? The man was set upon by thieves. I was probably one of them —

JESUS: — probably —

BARABBAS: — and then this guy —

JESUS: — a Samaritan —

BARABBAS: — this Samaritan helps him. What was the point of that one?

JESUS: That we are all brothers — even the hated Samaritan.

BARABBAS: Samaritans! You can have 'em. You know how many Samaritans it takes to change a light bulb? *(He sees Jesus shaking his head.)* Skip it.
   Okay. The parable about the guy who took his inheritance and blew it on high living. Then he came back, and his father received him and threw a big party for him. How about that one?

JESUS: God cares for those who are lost and then found.

BARABBAS: The one I never figured out was about the guys who worked in the vineyard. Some worked 12 hours, some eight hours, and some four hours; but they all got paid the same.

JESUS: That was about God's forgiveness. It is indivisible. You can't have 25 percent of it or 50 or 75 percent of it. You either have it all or none of it.

BARABBAS: Do I have God's love?

JESUS: It is your birthright as a human being.

BARABBAS: How about His forgiveness?

JESUS: You have only to ask for it.

BARABBAS: God-forgive-me. There. I asked for it. Am I forgiven?

JESUS: Did you mean it?

BARABBAS: No. I haven't done anything to be forgiven for. Men I've killed needed killing. I killed Mr. Lincoln, you know?

JESUS: Yes. I know.

BARABBAS: He went to a play that night. Him and his wife and Captain Whatshisname and his wife. They sat in the presidential box. Around 9:30 or so I snuck in behind him and let him have it in the back of the head with a Derringer. I jumped on the stage, yelling, *"Sic semper tyrannis!,"* but my foot tripped on the stupid flag, broke my leg and hobbled off and got away. It took him forever to die. They say it took until 7:30 the next morning. But he finally —

JESUS: That was a terrible thing you did, John Wilkes Booth.

BARABBAS: Was it? I killed the man that freed the slaves. What's wrong with that?

JESUS: He was mourned for a long time after that.

BARABBAS: By the slaves?

JESUS: By everyone.

BARABBAS: I did it. With my own hand, I did it. I, John Wilkes Booth. Does God love John Wilkes Booth?

JESUS: Did you ask him to, John Wilkes Booth?

BARABBAS: So we're supposed to love our enemies, huh? Even the Romans?

JESUS: Even the Romans.

BARABBAS: And we're supposed to turn the other cheek? Let's try it and see if it works. If I hit you on the cheek, will you turn the other also?

JESUS: Are you afraid it will work?

BARABBAS: Let's find out. *(He slaps Jesus.)* Aren't you going to turn the other also?

JESUS: It is turned.

BARABBAS: I'll wipe that smile off your face. *(He slaps him again. Jesus falls.)* There. It doesn't work, does it?

JESUS: Do it again.

BARABBAS: Are you daring me?

JESUS: No. I'm challenging you.

BARABBAS: All right. On your feet. *(As Jesus is getting up, Barabbas' attention is drawn to the cell door.)* At last! Grub! Mister, you've been saved by the well-known bell. What's this? The same old slop? I thought the prisoner's last meal was supposed to be special . . . What? . . . He said it wasn't my last meal. Must have gotten another reprieve. Here. This is your slop.

JESUS: I'm not hungry.

BARABBAS: I am. I've learned to eat this garbage, cockroaches and all. They're what give it body. Get it?

JESUS: Gallows humor again.

BARABBAS: Let me tell you my idea of a last meal. We start with nice little *hors d'oeuvres,* the kind high class dames serve at tea time. Then we polish off a piping hot bowl of potato soup. The next item is tossed salad with thousand island — check that, Waiter, make it blue cheese dressing. For the main course I'll have a big steak — New York cut, medium rare. And I'll wash it down with a tall bottle of French import. Let's say Bordeaux. I'm not done yet, but how do you like it so far?

JESUS: I liked the potato soup.

BARABBAS: Tell me, Jesus of Nazareth, Son of Joseph, what would you have for your last supper?

JESUS: I've already had it.

BARABBAS: What did you have?

JESUS: Bread and wine.

BARABBAS: Was that all?

JESUS: Those who had it with me will never hunger or thirst again.

BARABBAS: Who did you have it with?

JESUS: Twelve of my closest friends.

BARABBAS: I believe they're called disciples.

JESUS: Yes.

BARABBAS: Where are they now?

JESUS: Waiting.

BARABBAS: Waiting for what?

JESUS: To see what will happen to me.

BARABBAS: They know, don't they?

JESUS: They think they know.

BARABBAS: Since you're so good at making up parables, why don't you lay one on me? Do a parable for Brother Barabbas.

JESUS: There were two men who had been sentenced to exile from their native country. The governor gave each man a week in which to wind up his personal affairs.

The first man went to all his debtors and forgave them. Then he sold all he had and paid off his creditors. When the day came for him to sail away, he had no money, but a few of his friends came to weep and wish him farewell.

The second man went to all his debtors and demanded payment. If they couldn't pay up, he beat them. Then he went to money lenders and borrowed huge sums of money, not telling them he was going into exile and promising instead to pay them promptly.

When the day came for him to depart, there was no one there to weep for him or wish him farewell; so he went to his cabin and counted his money.

BARABBAS: And? . . . Well, does it just end there?

JESUS: There is an epilogue in the form of a question.

BARABBAS: Let's have it.

JESUS: Which of the two men was richer?

BARABBAS: That's easy. The one who counted his money.

JESUS: I suppose so.

BARABBAS: You're not sure? It was your story.

JESUS: The other one had friends, and when he was gone, both his former debtors and his creditors felt kindly toward him; so in a way, he was richer, too.

BARABBAS: Why do your stupid parables have to have a mystery connected with them?

JESUS: There is no mystery, Barabbas; for you and I are the men in the parable. Each of us is going into exile. When

22

I go, there will be a handful of friends who will weep for me. When you go down to the ship, who will weep for you, Barabbas? You will soon be free, but you will not be free. You will be in a cage of your own making. Your conscience will make bars for you such as the Romans could never have made.

BARABBAS: I have no conscience. You forget. I am what criminologists call a hardened criminal. They even have a fancy word for me. I'm a recidivist. Do you know what a recidivist is? A repeater. One who repeats his crimes and — hey! You're crying. Is Jesus of Nazareth afraid to die? I remember something else you said. You claimed you were the Son of God. Is the Son of God afraid to die?

JESUS: I long to be in paradise with my Father in heaven. But I weep for my people — my Jerusalem — for you, Barabbas.

BARABBAS: If you're really the Son of God, you can break us out of here. We don't need to trick the guard. What do you say?

JESUS: Do not tempt me, Barabbas, for to tempt me is to tempt God. *(Barabbas' attention is drawn to the other prisoners.)*

BARABBAS: What's that? . . . He wants us to shut up so he can sleep. In a few hours you'll get all the sleep you need. What did you call that? Gallows humor?

JESUS: Whatever.

BARABBAS: What? . . . Okay. The other guy wants to talk to you.

JESUS: Yes, Friend. What is it? . . . I don't think that can be arranged. . . . have courage, Friend. He wanted to be next to me when we go to — *(Barabbas has fallen asleep, but is tossing fitfully. Suddenly we go into a slow-motion dream sequence. Barabbas is kneeling at the side of his cot and stabbing at an imaginary body lying in it. He then goes to Jesus, showing him his bloody hands.)*

BARABBAS: There. I killed her.

JESUS: She was not someone who needed killing. She was bringing a baby — a new life — into the world.

BARABBAS: But who — was she?

JESUS: She was my mother.

BARABBAS: Let me look at her again. It's not her. It's you! It's Jesus of Nazareth! Kill! Kill! Kill! Kill! —

JESUS: It's all right, Barabbas. It's all right.

BARABBAS: I was dreaming.

JESUS: Yes.

BARABBAS: Who am I?

JESUS: A killer of innocents.

BARABBAS: Does God love a killer of innocents?

JESUS: Yes.

BARABBAS: Does God forgive a killer of innocents?

JESUS: Does he? *(Barabbas' attention is again drawn to the cell door.)*

BARABBAS: Well, what is it now, High Pockets? . . . Did you hear that? One of us is being released. Well, congratulations, Jesus of Nazareth. Now you can go back to your preaching about love . . . What? . . . Not him. Me? There's gotta be a mistake. I'm the guilty one. My friend here may be a little funny in the head, but he never hurt anyone.

JESUS: Whatever happened to the hardened criminal?

BARABBAS: I'm not sure I understand what's going on around here. I haven't understood a word you've said to me since High Pockets threw you in here a few minutes ago. All I know — I'm coming, I'm coming — is that you're going to hang, and I'm going free.

JESUS: There is no escape for you, Barabbas.

BARABBAS: Not one thing you've said to me has made sense. Not one thing. *(He exits.)*

JESUS: Father God, I pray for the soul and body of my friend Barabbas. He is crying out to you. In his crazy, violent way he is crying out to you. Only touch his heart and give him understanding — and forgiveness. A-men . . . Yes, I'm ready. My! He was right. You are tall, aren't you? *(Jesus exits. Presently Barabbas enters.)*

BARABBAS: Well, I'm home again. Only this time I'm innocent. Can you beat that? Barabbas innocent! They say I killed High Pockets. Well, he was dead — or nearly dead, and I stood over him with a dagger in my hand. What do you expect?

My three friends are all dead: Jesus of Nazareth and the two thieves. I went there to watch my old buddies die, but somehow I was drawn to Jesus on the cross. A few of his friends were there, and some women. I think one of them was his mother. They were exchanging words back and forth, but I couldn't make out what they were saying.

Then I did a strange thing. I reached up to Jesus. I don't know why. Maybe I thought he could reach back, but he couldn't. His hands were nailed. Then slowly he turned his head my way. He looked at me the way he used to look at me in the cell. I thought he was trying to say something to me, but all he did was nod his head.

Then the centurion who was in charge of the execution said to me: "You belong up there, Barabbas. Not him."

I turned and ran.

That was several days ago. All three of them are dead now. Oh, there are rumors that Jesus rose from the dead and appeared to some of his friends, but I don't believe those tales.

Do you?

Last night I was prowling the street when I stumbled on a body lying in the gutter. It was High Pockets. He had been set upon and beaten like the guy in the parable. I decided to have the honor of finishing him off; so I raised my dagger, and he opened his eyes and groaned. But I couldn't bring my hand down to kill him because when I looked at him, I found myself looking — into the face of Jesus.

THE END

Pontius Pilate And The Dreams Of Claudia

A One-Act Play
For Lent And
Good Friday

Program Notes

The purist who is concerned about historical accuracy will have a field day with this production.

It will be noted that the scene with Caiaphas and Pilate is historically impossible and the presence of Caiaphas at the trial of Christ historically false. No Jew of Caiaphas' standing would be caught dead in a pagan edifice such as the praetorium of a Roman governor.

The question could be asked: Why is the Angel of Death so sure about the comings and goings of Pontius Pilate and his wife? And what's all this jazz about Claudia Procula? The Matthew story does not give her name, nor does it appear anywhere in the Bible. The answer to all this is: After all, he should know. He's the Angel of Death.

So we have taken considerable poetic license (or dramatic license?) in presenting this fantasy. However, we have tried to capture the character of Pontius Pilate and the personality of his wife, Claudia Procula. We have tried to show the total illegality of Jesus' trials — both before the Sanhedrin and before Pilate. In doing so, we invite each member of each congregation to answer the question which Pilate asks himself: "What shall I do with this man who is called Christ?"

THE CAST
The Angel of Death
Pontius Pilate
Claudia Procula

Pontius Pilate And
The Dreams Of Claudia

(The Angel of Death appears on a stage which is bare except for two veiled statues standing side by side. The place is a church in no particular country, and the time is a moment in no particular century.)

ANGEL OF DEATH: I would like to welcome you all to this ceremony — this unveiling. You are indeed privileged to be here.

Oh! This is no ordinary unveiling, and these are two unique statues; for no one has ever erected statues of these two people before.

Who am I? It does not matter. Who I am is of no importance.

Well. Shall we proceed with the ceremony? Now, the first statue is of — What was that? You still wish to know who I am? You think me rude to stand up here and fail to identify myself? Very well, then.

I am the Angel of Death. Oh! Do not be frightened. You will not see me again for a generation — or two — or three — or, if you are very young and live a very long time, you may not see me again for four generations.

Now, where was I? Ah, yes. The ceremony — the unveiling. It is really a very simple ceremony. I will merely make a few remarks — introductory in nature. Then I will remove the veils in order that you may enjoy the workmanship, the art of these sculptures. I have seen them myself, and I can assure you they are very good — almost life-like in quality.

The first statue I am going to unveil is that of Pontius Pilate. It is the taller one of the two. Now, why, you ask, would anyone build a statue to Pontius Pilate?

Why, indeed! Do we not say his name with contempt whenever we mutter — pardon me, utter — the Creed of the Apostles: ". . . and suffered under Pontius Pilate?" So, why, then, a statue to this evil man? There is a reason, but we will come to that later. Let there be some suspense to this charade, or you will all take your leave and go home before I have dismissed you.

Did I say evil? This point has been argued by theologians and doctors for centuries. There is even a legend that he was beheaded by Nero and his body thrown into the Tiber River, but the Tiber would not accept his bones and spat them forth. He was then taken to the Rhone River where the Gauls lived, but the Rhone spat him up, too.

However, there are some churches which believe he confronted Jesus after the resurrection and that Jesus forgave him, that he became a follower of The Way and ultimately died a martyr to the church.

Pontius Pilate was governor of Judea, Sumaria and Idumia from 26 to 36 A.D. At the end of his governorship — or procuratorship, as the Romans called it, he was recalled to Rome for trial on a charge of incompetence. Before he got there, his friend, the Emperor Tiberius died, and Pilate was brought before the court of Caligula. He lived out his days in Gaul in exile, or — euphemistically — retirement.

What more is there to say? It was his fate to be in Jerusalem, in authority, during the Passover festival in the 30th year of Grace. That was the year that Jesus of Nazareth changed the course of world history.

I now unveil Pontius Pilate. There! You see? Very noble. Patrician. A Roman among Romans. And the other is his wife Claudia. I unveil her. Behold, the features of a true lady of Rome. It is written of her by the evangelist Matthew that she dreamed of Jesus before his trial and urged her husband to have nothing to do with him.

See how majestic they are? How life-like! What would they say to us if they were alive? How would you like to find out? I can do it, you know; for I am the Angel of Life. All I have to do is breathe the —

Ah! You have caught me. You heard me say I was the Angel of Death, and now you think I have contradicted myself by claiming to be the Angel of Life.

Well, I will let you in on a secret. I have the power of death *and* the power of life, and I might add that I am a very busy angel — as angels go. Many people have to die to make room for the many that have to be born.

Think on that for a moment, and while you are thinking on it, I will breathe life into the statue of Pontius Pilate. *(He breathes life into the Pilate statue.)*

PONTIUS PILATE: What am I doing here? Who are these people? I know you because I have met you before, but who are these people?

ANGEL: They are people who want you to talk to them.

PILATE: Why have you done this thing? My wife, Claudia Procula. Is she, too, alive?

ANGEL: Would you like her to be?

PILATE: Yes. Oh, yes! I am quite frightened of these surroundings. These people. What is this place? A temple?

ANGEL: You could say that.

PILATE: A cross. What a strange symbol! I hung many men on crosses like this one — only bigger and made of huge timbers. Claudia! You said you could bring her back to life.

ANGEL: I did.

32

PILATE: Then do it. *(The Angel breathes life into Claudia.)*

CLAUDIA PROCULA: My husband! *(They embrace.)*

PILATE: Yes. It is I. We have been restored to life for reasons that have not been explained to me.

CLAUDIA: What is this place?

PILATE: That is what I asked. It is a temple of some sort. Here. Let me show you something. What is this?

CLAUDIA: It is a symbol.

PILATE: Of what? of death? Are you people worshipers of death?

CLAUDIA: It is a symbol of life — of victory over death.

PILATE: You believe that?

CLAUDIA: I do not believe it. I know it.

PILATE: You — you brought us back to life. Perhaps you will unravel this mystery for us.

ANGEL: Gladly.

PILATE: Then, proceed. By all means, proceed.

ANGEL: Do you remember a Jesus of Nazareth?

PILATE: No.

ANGEL: He was a prophet from Galilee.

PILATE: Ah, yes. Prophets. We had them crawling out from every rock when I was procurator. A pesky lot!

ANGEL: You crucified him.

PILATE: He must have been guilty of sedition. I would have had no other reason to sentence him to death.

ANGEL: You found no fault in him, but you crucified him.

PILATE: Impossible!

CLAUDIA: It is true.

PILATE: You remember?

CLAUDIA: I dreamed of him one night. I warned you.

PILATE: Perhaps you will refresh my memory.

CLAUDIA: It was the time of the Jewish celebration called Passover. The Jews were commemorating their escape from Egypt in the ancient time —

PILATE: Never mind all that.

CLAUDIA: Jesus, the prophet from Galilee was in Jerusalem. Everyone was talking about him. People either loved him or hated him. Only the Romans were neutral. We neither knew, nor cared. There was talk that attempts would be made on his life; then the rumors stated that he would be brought before you, the procurator, and that you might give an official stamp to the —

PILATE: Where was I when all this was going on?

CLAUDIA: You were in Jerusalem.

PILATE: What was I doing in Jerusalem? The capital of the province was at Caesarea.

CLAUDIA: You always went to Jerusalem at Passover time. It was when the people were the most volatile and the city most restive. You said a firm hand was needed, and you had to be at the scene: to prevent violence, you said.

PILATE: This particular Passover. What year was it?

CLAUDIA: The fourth year of your procuratorship — the 16th of the reign of Tiberius.

PILATE: And this dream you had.

CLAUDIA: It was the night before you were to leave for Jerusalem. You were in your study, reading a letter. Your secretary announced me. *(The Angel at this point takes on the persona of Pilate's secretary.)*

SECRETARY: Your Excellency. Your wife wishes to speak to you.

PILATE: Send her in.

CLAUDIA: I would like a few words with you.

PILATE: Then speak, Claudia.

CLAUDIA: Alone. *(Pilate motions his secretary [the former Angel] to scram — which he does.)*

PILATE: Now, what is so important that you must interrupt my work?

CLAUDIA: I dreamed last night. It was a warning.

PILATE: As you can see, I am quite busy.

CLAUDIA: You will not heed my warning? You do not wish to hear it?

PILATE: I will hear it, by the gods, since by your demeanor I can tell you will give it to me whether I wish to hear it or not!

CLAUDIA: In my dreams a man stood before you.

PILATE: Who was this man?

CLAUDIA: I was not told his name. But one of his followers — a woman — thrust a crown in your hand. "Crown him," she said. "Crown him!" You took the crown, approached the man and said: "Would you wear this crown?" But he said nothing.

PILATE: What did he look like? This man on trial?

CLAUDIA: I could not see his face. His head was covered.

PILATE: Then what happened?

CLAUDIA: Then Caiaphas came forward. He was followed by an angry mob crying: "Crucify him! Crucify him!" You tried to quiet the people, but they kept pushing forward. Finally, you turned him over to them. Suddenly there was a great storm and an earthquake. When the excitement was over, there was great calm, and I looked up on a hill, and there was the man — hanging on a cross.

PILATE: A fascinating dream.

CLAUDIA: There is more. At the foot of the cross was a man crying out and screaming in remorse.

PILATE: Who was that man?

CLAUDIA: It was you.

PILATE: The reason your dream fascinates me is this letter I was reading when you came in. It is from this same Caiaphas who was in your dream. He writes Greek badly, but I know what he is trying to say. He speaks of a Jesus of Nazareth who claims linear descent from an ancient king of theirs named David. Jesus, he writes, intends to crown himself king of the Jews and lead an army against Rome. He will be present for the Passover, and I am to prepare my troops to fight off an armed attack.

CLAUDIA: This Jesus must be the one who appeared in my dream. You must have nothing to do with this man.

PILATE: I will deal with him as I must.

CLAUDIA: You will ignore my warning?

PILATE: Permit me to explain my understanding of Roman law. If this man were to kill a Roman citizen or steal from a Roman or lead a revolt against Rome or call for the overthrow of the Emperor Tiberius, then he would come under my jurisdiction, and it would be my duty to judge him according to Roman law. On the other hand, if his crime is against some other Jew or if he had transgressed some Jewish law, then his judgment will be in the jurisdiction of Caiaphas and the Sanhedrin of the Jews.

CLAUDIA: I fear for you, my husband.

PILATE: There is nothing to fear. We are Romans.

CLAUDIA: Now do you remember Jesus of Nazareth?

PILATE: I vaguely remember that conversation. And it is coming back to me now. I begin to recall that trial.

ANGEL: You received a visitor shortly after you arrived in Jerusalem.

PILATE: Who?

ANGEL: It was Caiaphas. I will need a robe for this. *(He borrows a robe from a choir member as Claudia stands off to the side of the stage.)*

PILATE: Who are these people?

ANGEL: The choir.

PILATE: The choir? And what function do they perform in this temple?

ANGEL: They sing songs.

PILATE: Strange looking people.

ANGEL: I am ready. *(He has donned the robe and a skull cap and has become Caiaphas.)*

PILATE: Ah, Caiaphas, my friend!

CAIAPHAS: Friend? I am hardly your friend, Your Excellency. Your subject, certainly. But not your friend.

PILATE: Your spoken Greek is more fluent than your written Greek.

CAIAPHAS: You sent for me.

PILATE: It concerns this Jesus of Nazareth. You wrote me about him.

CAIAPHAS: He is a trouble-maker.

PILATE: A trouble-maker for you, or a trouble-maker for Rome?

CAIAPHAS: If he were only our problem, I would not bother you about him.

PILATE: What sort of threat does he really pose?

CAIAPHAS: He would proclaim himself king of the Jews.

PILATE: Indeed!

CAIAPHAS: Only Caesar has the authority to appoint kings. That is your law.

PILATE: Tell me, Caiaphas, has he proclaimed himself king, or do you fear he might?

CAIAPHAS: Let me put it this way, Excellency. When he entered Jerusalem a few days ago, he was proclaimed king by the mob. He did not deny that he was a king.

PILATE: You call that evidence? Roman law requires more than that.

CAIAPHAS: He did not deny his kingship. Do not forget that.

PILATE: Tell me about this army he led into the city.

CAIAPHAS: Army?

PILATE: Surely, he must have had an army — if he was going to lead a revolt against Rome.

CAIAPHAS: He came riding on the back of a donkey.

PILATE: WHAT?!

CAIAPHAS: There was no army, but a huge crowd was there, cheering him on — throwing palm leaves in his path.

PILATE: This king of yours came riding into Jerusalem on the back of an ass! A mob threw greenery in his path! I am sure Tiberius the emperor is nervously pacing the palace floor, awaiting his forthcoming downfall!

CAIAPHAS: He urges the citizens not to pay taxes to Caesar, Your Excellency.

PILATE: You have the witnesses to this?

CAIAPHAS: Two witnesses.

PILATE: Were they cross-examined after they gave their testimony?

CAIAPHAS: What?

PILATE: I know something of your Jewish law. Not only must you have two witnesses to a crime, but each must be cross-examined separately afterward to ascertain if he corroborates the other's testimony.

CAIAPHAS: We — um — hardly thought that was necessary under the circumstances. There was a huge crowd present when he said that.

PILATE: Furthermore, if he transgressed Roman law, why was he tried for that in a Jewish court? I perceive, Caiaphas, that I may know more about your law than you do.

CAIAPHAS: I do not understand you, Your Excellency. We have a defendant for you in our custody. He is as much a threat to your institutions as he is to ours. And yet you stand there and quibble over technical points of law.

PILATE: Caiaphas, I once respected you as the leader of a subject population. My feeling for you is now one of contempt.

CAIAPHAS: How you feel about me is of no importance to me, Excellency. But if you fail to take measures against this man, you will be no friend of Caesar.

PILATE: I am sure that Caesar has confidence in my word and in my administration.

CAIAPHAS: Will his confidence be enhanced if he learns that you are unable to handle the rioting that may occur if you fail to carry out the will of the people who demand this man's execution?

PILATE: I do not succumb to threats. Tiberius, the Emperor, is a personal friend.

CAIAPHAS: You have already offended my people three times. First, by placing Roman battle standards in the Holy City. Second, by taking money from our treasury to build an aquaduct. And third, by butchering those who refused to build it. Do you wish to commit a fourth offense against the Jews?

PILATE: Whom I offend or do not offend in the carrying out of my duty is irrelevant, Caiaphas. But you have piqued my curiosity. Bring forth this prisoner of yours. Let me make the ultimate determination and put forward the final verdict.

CAIAPHAS: I will bring him forth as you wish, Your Excellency. But in the background give ear to the voices that are crying: "Crucify him! Crucify him!"

PILATE: Roman law was not written to be amended by the howling of a subject race. Bring him. *(An imaginary Jesus stands before Pilate.)* Are you Jesus of Nazareth? . . . What manner of man is this, Caiaphas? He does not answer.

CAIAPHAS: Question him further.

PILATE: Are you the king of the Jews? . . . I do not understand Aramaic. Translate.

CAIAPHAS: He said, "You have said so."

PILATE: What does that mean?

CAIAPHAS: I think it means yes. By the same token, it could mean no.

PILATE: I ask you again: Are you the king of the Jews? . . . Translation, please.

CAIAPHAS: He wants to know if you ask him this of your own accord, or have others spoken to you about him?

PILATE: Am I a Jew? It is your own people and your own Sanhedrin who have handed you over to me. What have you done? . . .

CAIAPHAS: He said: "My kingdom is not of this world. If it were, my men would have fought to prevent my being surrendered to the Jews."

PILATE: Then you admit you are a king? . . .

CAIAPHAS: "I am a king. I was born to this. I came into the world for this: to bear witness to the truth." Now you have your evidence, Pontius Pilate. What will you do with it?

PILATE: Truth?! What is the truth? . . .

CAIAPHAS: Now he says that he is the truth and that all who are on the side of the truth will listen to his voice.

PILATE: You are the truth!? . . . I find no case against this man. He may have broken some law of yours, but he has committed no crime against Rome. I have reached my verdict: he is innocent.

CAIAPHAS: That cannot be! Are you deaf to the voices in the street? "Crucify him! Crucify him!" they cry. Are you to ignore the voice of the people?

PILATE: Will it please the people if I have him flogged?

CAIAPHAS: There is no place for compromise.

PILATE: What, then, shall I do with this man who is called Christ?

CAIAPHAS: You hear them: "Crucify him! Crucify him!"

PILATE: But he is innocent of any crime against Rome.

CAIAPHAS: He is guilty of crimes against our faith.

PILATE: Then let your faith put him to death, and let his blood be on you.

CAIAPHAS: We cannot do that, for it is contrary to our laws. It must be your decision.

PILATE: I have a solution that will no doubt satisfy all concerned. It has become the custom during Passover to free a prisoner who is condemned to death. There is Jesus Barabbas — guilty of sedition and murder. There is Jesus of Nazareth who you say has transgressed your laws. What say you? Which shall I set free?

CAIAPHAS: Barabbas! The people would have you release Barabbas and crucify Jesus of Nazareth.

PILATE: Very well, as you wish. Take him away, and release Barabbas. Let the prophet hang. Bring forth water that I may wash my hands of the blood of this innocent man. *(Caiaphas removes his robe and skull cap and becomes the Angel of Death again.)*

ANGEL: You thought by washing your hands in a basin of water you could absolve yourself of guilt?

PILATE: There is still blood on my hands.

CLAUDIA: I see none.

ANGEL: Nor I.

PILATE: But I see it.

CLAUDIA: If you had heeded the warning of my dream —

PILATE: If the great Caesar had heeded the warning of Calpurnia's dream on the eve of the Ides of March, he would not have died under the daggers of the assassins.

ANGEL: But because you did not heed the warning, you committed an offense against justice that brought eternal infamy to your name.

PILATE: I was in the wrong place at the wrong moment of history.

ANGEL: Were you? You asked Caiaphas and the mob: "What shall I do with this man who is called Christ?" Every generation since — every man, woman and child who has reached the age of discretion has had to answer that question.

PILATE: I answered it my way. How have you answered it? Did you betray him as one did or deny him as some did or did you run and hide? I called for a basin of water to wash the blood from my hands. You do not see it, but I see it. You do not know the extent of my guilt, but I know it. *(Pilate stands off to the side of the stage.)*

CLAUDIA: I was often given to dreams.

ANGEL: Did they always come true?

CLAUDIA: Some did. Some did not. But there was one — a special one. It followed me all my life.

ANGEL: Would you like to tell us about it?

CLAUDIA: You would not want to hear it. It made no sense to me, and I am sure it will make none to you.

ANGEL: Let us decide that after you have told us.

CLAUDIA: It first came to me when I was a little girl in Rome. Augustus was still emperor then. I was wandering — alone — in a far off country. I did not know where it was, but I now know it must have been Judea where my future husband would some day be procurator. It was cold and dark, and I seemed drawn to a little town. Soon others joined me, and we were all searching for something, but we did not know what it was. Finally, we came to a stable. There were people in it. I heard a baby crying. Then I woke up.

ANGEL: You had this dream several times?

CLAUDIA: The next time was when my husband had just been appointed procurator, and we knew we would be leaving Rome in a few days. It was so real! I had to ask my husband if he, too, had heard a baby crying.

ANGEL: It was exactly the same dream?

CLAUDIA: Yes. Always the same. I dreamed it several more times. There was always a cold night. The people moving with me. But the last time I dreamed it, it was different.

45

ANGEL: When was that?

CLAUDIA: I was an old woman. My husband had retired, and we moved to Gaul, to a place called the Valley of the Vineyards. He had died a few years before I dreamed it for the last time.

ANGEL: How was it different?

CLAUDIA: This time I was allowed to see the baby. His mother and father were by his side. They motioned to me to come forward and take him in my arms. I picked up the child, and he stopped crying. I held him close to me. A strange warmth came over me. I kissed him.

ANGEL: And then —

CLAUDIA: Then you came for me. *(The Angel takes Claudia by the hand and helps her mount her statue base. Then he does the same for Pilate. They become statues again.)*

ANGEL: I suppose you deserve an epilogue. You shall have one. We build a statue to Pontius Pilate because he represents all that is good and bad in man: the knowledge of what is good and the capacity in spite of that knowledge to do bad. Shall we condemn this man? No. It is not ours to condemn. For who of us can affirm that if he had been in Pilate's sandals, in Pilate's toga, in the praetorium in Jerusalem, in the 16th year of the reign of Tiberius Caesar that he would not have done the same thing.

   And Claudia? Claudia Procula? She deserves a statue in her own right. She was pure and noble and the first Pagan in high position to commit herself to the new faith.

   And now, before they become frozen in stone, permit me a final gesture. *(He joins their hands and bows to the congregation.)*

THE END

www.ingramcontent.com/pod-product-compliance
Lightning Source LLC
Chambersburg PA
CBHW060943050426
42453CB00009B/1111